IMAGES
of England

SALTLEY, DUDDESTON AND NECHELLS

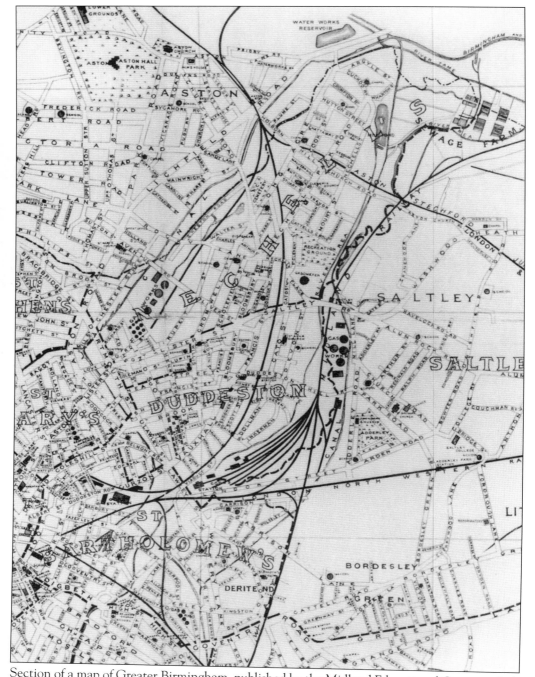

Section of a map of Greater Birmingham, published by the Midland Educational Company Ltd, around 1894, showing the Saltley, Duddeston and Nechells area of Birmingham.

IMAGES
of England

SALTLEY, DUDDESTON
AND NECHELLS

Compiled by
Maria Twist

TEMPUS

First published 2001
Copyright © Maria Twist, 2001

Tempus Publishing Limited
The Mill, Brimscombe Port,
Stroud, Gloucestershire, GL5 2QG

ISBN 0 7524 2279 0

Typesetting and origination by
Tempus Publishing Limited
Printed in Great Britain by
Midway Colour Print, Wiltshire

Mr Henry Matthews addressing the electors at Nechells Green, 1892. Matthews had been elected MP for East Birmingham in 1886 and became Home Secretary in the same year. He was the first Roman Catholic to become a cabinet minister since the passing of the Emancipation Act in 1829.

Contents

Acknowledgements

All the photographs in this book are from the collections in the Local Studies and History Service of Birmingham Library Services. The lower photograph on p. 44, both photographs on p. 45 and the top photograph on p. 56 are reproduced by courtesy of the *Birmingham Post and Mail* Ltd. I should like to thank my husband, Frank Twist, for his unfailing support during the compilation of this book and my sister, Fran Jones, for her help. I am also grateful to the Heartlands Local History Society, and in particular Diane Woodhouse and Eric Hill, who have kindly supplied information from their own local knowledge as background to some of the photographs. I should also like to thank Martin Flynn, Central Library Manager, and my colleagues in the Local Studies and History Service for their continued support.

Birmingham from the railway at Saltley, 1840. Birmingham's first two railway lines can be seen in this picture. The London to Birmingham Railway, opened in 1838, passes under the bridge in the foreground, while the train in the distance is on the Grand Junction Railway, opened in 1837. Curzon Street station, still standing today, can be seen in the background.

Introduction

Saltley, Duddeston and Nechells form the north-eastern sector of Birmingham's inner city. Known rather for its industrial landscapes and its poverty, there are few grand buildings or fine houses to be seen here. Yet generations of Birmingham people have lived and worked here and many still feel affection for its schools, pubs and workplaces and the sense of community in its overcrowded courts and terraces. This selection of photographs, spanning more than a century, will hopefully give an insight into the past of the area, which has its own interest and fascination but few claims to beauty.

Most of Saltley, Duddeston and Nechells falls within the present Nechells ward, although it spills over into Washwood Heath ward on the eastern side. The manors of Saltley, Duddeston and Nechells were part of the large Warwickshire parish of Aston. Duddeston and Nechells were included in Birmingham when it achieved borough status in 1838, while Saltley remained in Warwickshire for the time being. Saltley Local Board of Health was formed in 1872, becoming an Urban District in 1888 and eventually part of the City of Birmingham in 1891.

The Holte family had been associated with Duddeston at least since the thirteenth century and purchased the manors of Duddeston, Nechells and Aston in the fourteenth century. Duddeston Hall, commemorated in Duddeston Hall Road, was the seat of the Holtes until Sir Thomas Holte went to live in his new mansion, Aston Hall, in 1631. The last member of the Holte family to live there was the Dowager Lady Holte who died in 1738. The Hall was then sold and the estate developed into a pleasure garden called Vauxhall Gardens – after those in London – which continued until 1850, when the land was sold for building purposes. William Hutton's daughter, Catherine, and her mother stayed at Vauxhall after their house at Bennett's Hill was damaged in the Church and King Riots of 1791. Catherine described Vauxhall as '...a kind of tavern, with a bowling green, orchestra, woods and walks, and during the summer a public night once a week, on which there are musical performances.'

The part of Duddeston nearest to the town centre of Birmingham had been planned as the 'hamlet of Ashted' in the late eighteenth and early nineteenth centuries and was advertised as a healthy and convenient place to live. An early example of town planning, Ashted must have been an elegant and fashionable suburb in its day. At this time, Nechells and Saltley were still sparsely populated rural areas with scattered farms and mills on the River Rea and Aston Brook, which both flowed northwards to join the River Tame. Although there must have been a Nechells Manor House, it disappeared so long ago that there is no record of it. The rather strange name of Nechells probably means 'separate estate' or an addition to an existing estate.

The name Saltley means 'clearing amongst the willow trees' which sounds attractive. In 1997, archaeologists discovered traces of a lost medieval village under demolished houses in Saltley, consisting of about twenty timber houses. It was thought to have been abandoned in the fifteenth century. Even as late as the mid-nineteenth century Saltley was described as 'a small bridge over the River Rea, the osier beds that lined the flat low road to the village ... the turnpike gate, enormous Lombardy poplars, beeches, oaks, meadows and shady lanes.' Such a rural scene is now very difficult to imagine. Saltley Hall was built in the seventeenth century by the Adderley family, but replaced an earlier hall which was remembered locally as 'Giant's Castle.' The Adderley family lived at Hams Hall a few miles away rather than at Saltley and from the eighteenth century the Hall was let to farmers.

Charles Bowyer Adderley, the first Lord Norton, was responsible for developing Saltley as a suburb from the mid-nineteenth century. He also gave the land for the building of Saltley Training College and Saltley Reformatory.

The Birmingham and Fazeley Canal and the Digbeth Branch Canal had been completed in 1790 and these gave the impetus to the growth of industry in the area. Birmingham's first two railway lines also crossed the area, firstly the Grand Junction Railway from Liverpool in 1837 and secondly the

London to Birmingham Railway in 1838, both eventually terminating at Curzon Street station, until the more centrally placed New Street station was completed in 1852. In 1842, the Birmingham and Derby Junction Railway was added to the network and other branches were added later so that the whole area is criss-crossed by a complex railway system. This gave rise to one of the main industries, which was railway carriage and wagon manufacture. Good transport links also contributed to the establishment of gas works in Nechells and Saltley and later the Nechells power station, all needing plentiful supplies of coal. As the 'powerhouse' of Birmingham, Nechells and Saltley acquired their distinctive industrial landscapes, which made them unattractive and unhealthy places in which to live. Duddeston and Nechells have suffered from acute housing problems throughout as there were never enough good houses built at rents which poor people could afford. In spite of several redevelopment schemes, these problems largely remain.

Saltley, Duddeston and Nechells have not produced many people who have become well known. However, it is interesting that Birmingham's first woman MP, Mrs Edith Wills, represented Duddeston in Parliament and also lived in the area. She was elected in 1945 as a Labour MP and was the wife of an engine driver who lived in Rupert Street. A supporter of the Co-operative Movement, she was the ideal person to represent a working-class area of the city.

Duddeston and Nechells have now become an important part of Birmingham's regeneration programme. Aston University, Birmingham's second of three universities, and the nearby Science Park, fall within its boundaries. The Millenium Point development, which includes the new Science Museum, is nearing completion. The Heartlands and Waterlinks projects have brought more industry to the area again and have involved building a new access road, now completed. With the coming of ambitious projects such as these, the residential population of Nechells and Washwood Heath wards has been in decline, although some new housing has been built. There seems to be an exciting future ahead for this part of Birmingham and hopefully, scenes of industrial decay will soon be a thing of the past.

All the photographs in this book are from the extensive collections in the Local Studies and History Service of Birmingham Library Services. Some are by Sir Benjamin Stone, whose magnificent photograph collection is one of the library's prize possessions. The collections are continually being expanded and the library is always eager to receive photographs donated by the public. Photographs can be copied and returned if donors wish to retain the originals.

Horse tram at Nechells, 1906. This was the last year in which horse trams ran in Birmingham, where they had been in use rather longer than in most other towns.

One
Ashted and
Gosta Green

Ashted Row with a view of Mr Green's house, 1895. Mr Green was one of the partners in Bacchus and Green's glass works, afterwards Stone, Fawdry and Stone of Union Glass Works, Dartmouth Street. Sir Benjamin Stone, who took some of the photographs in this book, was one of the proprietors, along with his father.

The corner of Willis Street and Ashted Row, c. 1960. Ashted was named after Dr John Ash, physician to the General Hospital, who built himself a mansion there in 1777. In 1787 an attorney called John Brooke acquired forty-one acres on the Holte Estate to develop as a residential suburb. One of his sub-developers was a builder called William Windsor. These names all appear in street names in the area.

Ashted Row, 11 November 1952. These houses with their air of faded elegance indicate that Ashted was once a fashionable suburb. Building plots had been advertised as 'very inviting to ladies and gentlemen wanting a pleasing retirement' and 'not likely to be surrounded by buildings.' Rather incongruously, there were also 'many advantageous situations for manufactures and other business.'

Ashted Row, 12 September 1961.

Ashted Row, March 1961.

Ashted Row, 16 February 1961. The old houses have fallen into disrepair and are gradually giving way to small workshops and businesses.

Ashted Place, 1950s. The ornamental wrought-iron sign above the entrance to this old court with its uneven cobbles lends it an almost romantic charm.

Heneage Street, *c.* 1961. Many of the street names in the Ashted area reflect its origins as part of the estate of the Holte family and its successors. Heneage Legge, who inherited the Holte estate after the Holtes died out, gave his name to Heneage and Legge Streets.

Heneage Street, *c.* 1961. These back-to-back houses with outside toilets and washhouses, were typical nineteenth-century dwellings in the area.

The corner of Heneage Street and Henry Street, April 1945. The building with the arched windows is occupied by C.T. Willetts Ltd, domestic hardware manufacturers. The same family had been in business there for at least a hundred years.

Lawrence Street, c. 1970. The houses in Ryder Street and Lawrence Street were the first municipal houses built in Birmingham, in 1889 and 1891 respectively. They were demolished in 1971, but some of the terracotta plaques featuring the city's coat of arms survive on the Aston University campus.

Great Lister Street, March 1960.

Coleshill Street looking from Duke Street towards Dale End, around 1914. These three-storey houses probably date from the early nineteenth century.

Coleshill Street, Prospect Row and Aston and Birmingham Row from near Market Street, 1940s. The Second World War poster on the right of the photograph gives a clue to the date of the photograph.

Coleshill Street from the south west of Doe Street, looking north east, 1940s. The sign just visible on the post on the left points to a British Restaurant. These were designed to provide meals for people who were not able to take meals at home because of war-time conditions, transport difficulties and so on.

A.B. Row, 12 August 1932. A.B. Row was given the name as it marked the boundary between the parishes of Aston and Birmingham.

A.B. Row and the corner of Prospect Row, 18 June 1963. The building with tall arched windows was the old Gosta Green market hall, erected in 1837. The house at the front is thought to have been called Prospect House, where the market superintendent resided.

Gosta Green, early 1930s. Gosta Green, once Upper and Lower Gorsty Green, was given this name because of the gorse bushes which grew on the heathland which once covered the area. This photograph shows the site of the central fire station on a wintry day. The streets of houses, shops and small businesses have now gone and the rest of the site is occupied by Aston University.

Gosta Green, September 1937. A view of the same site after the completion of the central fire station. The newly-planted roundabout is still criss-crossed with tramlines.

18

Gosta Green, summer 1950. On the left is the Delicia cinema, at this period being used to stage wrestling matches. The Sacks of Potatoes pub is still standing and is much frequented by students from nearby Aston University.

Adams Street, 1935. George V's Silver Jubilee is being celebrated in this street party.

Aston Street, 5 February 1937. Both the street and pavements are laid with brick-shaped cobbles, known as setts and usually made of granite.

Aston Street, 11 February 1932. The horse-drawn cart is perhaps making a delivery of bread to the baker's shop on this wet and miserable day.

Fisher Street, c. 1900. The building on the corner is a pub called the Dog & Pheasant run by Holders Brewery, one of several local breweries which used good quality water from artesian wells. The three-storey houses built in the late eighteenth and early nineteenth centuries are in a poor state of repair and many were soon to be swept away.

The Aston end of Gem Street, c. 1912-13. The woman holding the baby is Mrs Scott. The shop window shows an enticing display of sweets and groceries.

Legge Street, *c*. 1900. These old houses have 'To Let' signs on them, but do not look very inviting.

The Copestick family having afternoon tea, 1930s. Joseph Copestick's shop was at 117 Henry Street, so this photograph may have been taken in the yard behind the shop.

Two
Industry

Duddeston Flour Mill, 1864. Originally the manorial cornmill of the Holte family, it was occupied by Robert Evans in 1864. In the 1740s it was leased to Joseph Farmer, whose daughter Mary married the Quaker gunmaker Samuel Galton. Galton used the mill for his gun-making business and so fell foul of the Quaker community in Birmingham.

Park Mills and pool, Nechells, 1896. At this time, the mill was occupied by the edge-tool works of Messrs Wills.

The mill pool at Park Mills, February 1896. St Clement's vicarage is in the centre background, the residence at this time of the Revd J.T. Butlin. Roland Stone, the son of the photographer Sir Benjamin Stone, is standing on the bank path. The pool is now filled in and Mount Street Recreation Ground occupies the site.

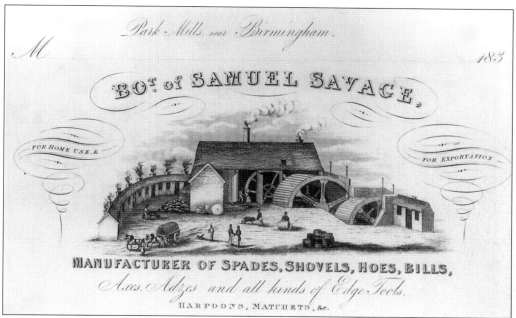

Park Mills billhead, 1830s.

Union Glass Works, Dartmouth Street, 1895. Owned by Stone, Fawdry and Stone, this was one of the sources of the wealth of Sir Benjamin Stone which enabled him to pursue his photographic and political interests.

Union Glass Works, Dartmouth Street, 1892.

Union Glass Works, Dartmouth Street, 1892. The furnaces used to produce the glass are seen in this view.

Showroom of Union Glass Works, 1890.

Design for a glass palace by the architect J.A. Chatwin, 1907. The design was produced in 1881 for the Maharajah Sindhia of Gwalior in the Sindh province of India, but it was never actually built.

Union Paper Mills, Landor Street, June 1895. The firm of Smith, Stone and Knight was founded in 1862 and was the other main business interest of Sir Benjamin Stone. Thomas Bird Smith and Benjamin Stone married two sisters, Jane and Ann Parker, and the other partner, Frederick Knight, married Stone's sister Clara, so it was a real family concern. The firm made the coarser kinds of paper such as wrapping and corrugated paper and that used for paper bags. Smith, Stone and Knight are still in existence in Mount Street, Nechells.

Clerks at Smith, Stone and Knight's paper mills, 1895.

Bag makers at Smith, Stone and Knight's paper mills, 1895.

The old bag room at Smith, Stone and Knight's paper mills, 1895.

Rag sorters at Smith, Stone and Knight's paper mills, 1895.

Machine room at Smith, Stone and Knight's paper mills, 1895. These young boys are cutting sheets of paper, which must have been a rather hazardous operation.

Machine room at Smith, Stone and Knight's paper mills, 1895.

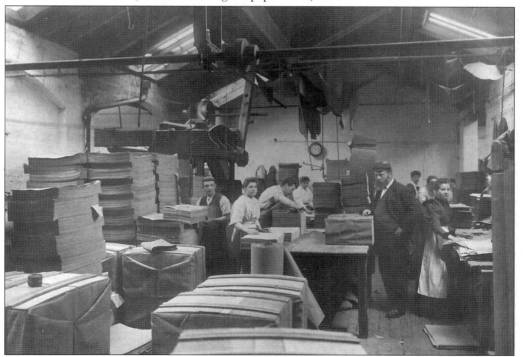

The Sol (*Salle*) at Smith, Stone and Knight's paper mills, 1895. The packing of the finished paper is being carried out here.

The Sol (*Salle*) at Smith, Stone and Knight's paper mills, 1894.

'Sol girls' at Smith, Stone and Knight's paper mills, 1895.

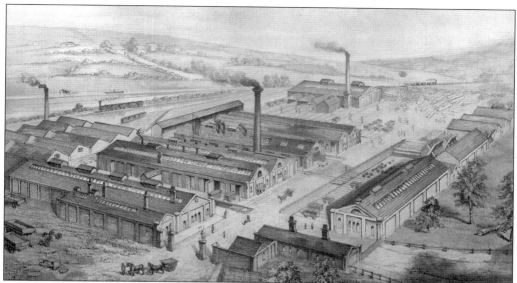

J. Wright and Sons, railway carriage and wagon works, Saltley, 1858. This view is from the *New Illustrated Directory*, published by M. Billing, a Birmingham lithographer. Joseph Wright, a coachbuilder from London, founded his railway carriage works at Saltley in 1845 on a site adjoining the Birmingham and Derby Junction Railway's Birmingham extension of 1842. After amalgamating with several other firms, it became the famous Metro-Cammell works, which made carriages and wagons for railways and tramways worldwide. Joseph Wright died in 1859 and the business was continued by his two sons, Henry and Joseph.

Visit of HRH Duke Tsai Tse to the Metropolitan Works, Saltley, 14 May 1906. The Chinese visitors saw carriages being made for the Shanghai and Nankin Railway.

Joseph Wright, founder of the Metropolitan Works, Saltley. This photograph and the one opposite are portraits by an unknown artist.

Mrs Wright, wife of Joseph Wright.

Birmingham Railway Carriage and Wagon Co. Ltd, early 1900s. The Works Ambulance Corps, holders of the Beck Challenge Cup, are shown in this photograph.

King George V inspecting gun carriages at Saltley during the First World War.

King George V inspecting works at Saltley during the First World War. It is not certain whether these photographs show the Metropolitan Works or some other works in the area which had been diverted to war work

Old engine houses at Fazeley Street Mills, November 1893.

Copper mill at Fazeley Street Mills, November 1893.

Silver mill and part of old mill at Fazeley Street Mills, November 1893.

Birmingham Paper Mills, Cattells Grove, in the early twentieth century.

Workers at Saltley Dock, *c*. 1894. Boats were built and repaired here at the workshops of Fellows, Morton and Clayton by these craftsmen and labourers. They were described as tarpaulers, carpenters, sawyers and painters.

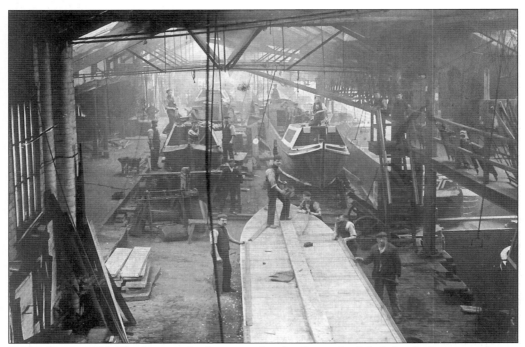

Saltley Dock, 1903. The boat in the foreground is the *Egypt* which left the dock on completion on 18 December 1903.

Delta Metals children's outing, 1930s. This was organized by Delta Metals in conjunction with St Lawrence's church to give local children a much-needed treat. The destination is unknown, but outings were often to local beauty spots such as Sutton Park or the Lickey Hills.

Windsor Street Gas Works, probably in the 1920s. Originally run by a private company called the Birmingham Gas Light and Coke Company, founded in 1819, these works were taken over by Birmingham Corporation in 1875 as a result of Joseph Chamberlain's plan to establish municipal gas and water undertakings.

An aerial view of Windsor Street Gas Works, 1930s. Railway sidings and arms from the Birmingham and Fazeley Canal ran alongside the gas works.

Women workers at Nechells Gas Works during the First World War. Originally part of Saltley Gas Works, Nechells became a separate works in 1900. The first gas holders on the site had been erected in 1881. These women were doing what would have been men's work in normal times.

Gas explosion at Saltley Gas Works, Duddeston Mill Road, 10 October 1904. Saltley Gas Works were first laid out in 1858 by the Birmingham and Staffordshire Gas Light Company and were transferred to Birmingham Corporation in 1875.

Saltley Gas Works looking towards Snow Hill station, 1930s.

Pickets in the early morning chill at Nechells power station, 30 November 1959. Birmingham's Electric Supply Department had built Nechells Power Station in 1915 to provide extra power for the war effort. After the war it was developed into a permanent station, officially opened in 1923 by the Prince of Wales. As a result, it was often known as Prince's Station. The strike in 1959 was a twenty-four-hour token stoppage by 350 manual workers in support of an hours and holidays claim. (Copyright, *Birmingham Post and Mail* Ltd)

Nechells Power Station from Salford Bridge, *c.* 1961. (Copyright, *Birmingham Post and Mail* Ltd)

Nechells Power Station, 10 October 1973. A luncheon party was held in the new main outfall sewer underneath the power station to show that it was clean enough to eat in. It was the idea of the managing director of Sheridan's, the Birmingham contractors, who carried out the work. A similar lunch marked the opening of the original sewer at the turn of the nineteenth century. The entertainment complex called Star City now stands on this site. (Copyright, *Birmingham Post and Mail* Ltd)

Dartmouth Street, 25 October 1957. This was the first flatted factory in Birmingham, being let to a number of firms each having their own 'flat' within the building. The architect was Philip Skelcher in association with Birmingham's City Architect. A corner of Dartmouth Street School can be seen on the right.

Another view of the Dartmouth Street flatted factory, 22 October 1957.

Three
Schools and Colleges

Back view of Saltley Training College, 1868. St Peter's College, Saltley was opened as Worcester Diocesan Training School in 1852. Part of a national movement to train teachers in an effort to improve the education of the poor, it continued to do so until its closure in 1978. The building is still in existence and is currently being used for residential purposes.

Front view of Saltley Training College, 1868.

The quadrangle of Saltley Training College, c. 1890.

Saltley Training College extensions, 1911/12.

Saltley Training College extensions, 1911/12. The new recreation room is shown in this photograph, below.

Saltley Reformatory, Fordrough Lane, 1903. Saltley Reformatory had its origins in an institution in Ryland Road, Birmingham, founded by Joseph Sturge. Charles Bowyer Adderley (later Lord Norton) of Hams Hall, Warwickshire, provided five acres of land at Saltley for a larger home and working farm for young offenders, which opened in 1853 with twenty-five boys. The Reformatory later became known as Norton Training School and eventually moved to Kineton in Warwickshire.

A young inmate of Saltley Reformatory, 1890.

Bloomsbury Girls' School, Dartmouth Street, 7 September 1964. The building in this photograph is the former Dartmouth Street School, opened in 1876. Bloomsbury Girls' School moved there in 1954 from its original building in Lingard Street, which had been built in 1873 and was the first Board School built by the Birmingham School Board. The Lingard Street building closed in 1968 and was demolished. A plaque marks the site today.

Loxton Street School, Nechells Green, 12 November 1964. This school was opened in 1883.

Nechells Primary School, Eliot Street, December 1974. This school was opened in 1879 as Hutton Street Board School. After proposals to close the school in the 1970s, parents, pupils and teachers fought to keep. it open and it was reprieved.

Nechells Primary School, Eliot Street, December 1974. This interior view shows typical School Board architecture. Many of the Board Schools were designed by the architects Martin and Chamberlain.

Nechells Park Road School, 5 July 1973. Charles Arthur Street Council School, opened in 1911, was the original name of this school.

Nechells Park Road School, 5 July 1973.

Tilton Road School, 20 January 1973. Tilton Road Board School opened in 1891.

Tilton Road School, 20 January 1973.

Saltley Grammar School, Belcher's Lane. This well-known grammar school opened in 1928 and had a very high reputation among Birmingham grammar schools. The school still exists but is no longer a grammar school.

Ashted Classical and Commercial School

Ashted Classical and Commercial School in the early nineteenth century. No doubt opened to cater for the new residents of Ashted, this school has left no trace of its history behind.

The opening of the new Aston Technical College by Queen Elizabeth II, 3 November 1955. First opened as Birmingham Municipal Technical School in 1895, it was designated the first College of Advanced Technology in the country on 24 September 1956. A university charter was granted in 1966 and the College became Aston University, Birmingham's second university. (Copyright, *Birmingham Post and Mail* Ltd)

Gosta Green Library fountain in its original position. The fountain stood outside Gosta Green Library, which was opened on 1 February 1868. It now stands near Waterstones bookshop.

Four
Halls and Houses

Duddeston House, 1868. Samuel Galton built this house for himself and his family near Duddeston Mill. The house was built in 1777 and later became an asylum. From 1868 it housed St Anne's School, but it has now been demolished.

Duddeston House, 1868.

Old Park House, Park Street, *c.* 1890.

Old house at No. 17 Bloomsbury Street, Nechells. This house must once have been a very desirable residence with its elegant balcony and railings. In the 1930s it was occupied by the City of Birmingham Maternity and Infantile Welfare Centre.

Ashted House, Ashted Row, 18 August 1932. This was a true Georgian house built about 1790, which stood on the corner of Ashted Row and Great Lister Street. By this time, many of the old houses had fallen into disrepair and most disappeared and were replaced by new housing or small businesses.

A Georgian house at No. 205 Vauxhall Road, 14 March 1958. The house was occupied at this time by the City of Birmingham Welfare Department.

Old farm house off Great Lister Street, 1896. Formerly Farmer Garbutt's, it was later occupied by the Perkins family.

Nechells Park, 1892. This house was probably near Nechells Park Mills and may have been the house called Park House on the Ordnance Survey map of 1889, situated between Nechells Park Road and Mount Street. The site is now a recreation ground referred to locally as 'The Old Ladies' Park'.

The back of Nechells Park, 1892.

Nechells Manor House, 1897. This house is marked as 'Manor House' on the Ordnance Survey map of 1889 and was on the southern side of Chattaway Street near the corner of Cook Street. There seems to be no evidence of an earlier manor house in Nechells.

Saltley Hall, 1896. In later times known as Jenkins' Farm, the site of Saltley Hall was to the north-west of Hall Road.

The house of the historian, William Hutton, at Bennett's Hill, Saltley, 1896. The house was damaged and set on fire during the Church and King Riots in Birmingham in 1791. William Hutton was Birmingham's first historian.

Bennett's Hill House, February 1896. William Hutton built this house in 1810 for his son, Thomas, opposite his own house. His daughter Catherine, who was also an author, lived there until her death in 1846.

Bennett's Hill House.

Bennett's Hill House.

Two
Duddeston and Nechells

Mr Henry Matthews' Committee Rooms, 1892 during the Parliamentary Election campaign for East Birmingham.

Duddeston Conservative Club, Vauxhall Road, 1895. Edward Bagley, Secretary of the East Birmingham Conservative Association, is standing at the door.

House at Nechells near the railway bridge, General Election, 1892. The house is covered with Mr Matthews' election bills. The Kelsey family formerly lived in the house.

Numbers 130-135 Great Brook Street and 104-116 Windsor Street, *c.* 1905.

Great Brook Street, 1895. Sir Benjamin Stone was born in the house on the right next to the railings in 1838.

Lupin Street, 1895. The second house on the left was built by Sir Benjamin Stone's father. The family lived there from 1840 until they moved to Sutton Street, Aston.

Lupin Street, 1896.

Numbers 30 and 34 Windsor Street, c. 1905. Many of the photographs in this section of the book are from around 1905 when a slum clearance scheme was in progress. Some houses were demolished, while others were renovated. This photograph shows an entrance opened up from the street to a court of houses at the rear. The walls have been topped with some very decorative railings. Opening up the court was one way of introducing more light and air to the houses at the back.

Numbers 1 and 2 at the rear of Nos 52 and 54 Midland Street, c. 1905. These were back-to-back houses, which had been condemned as insanitary in the 1890s, although many continued to be lived in until the latter half of the twentieth century. The death rates in such houses were much higher than in better-quality housing.

Numbers 1 and 2 in 6 Court, New Canal Street, *c.* 1905. This photograph shows a court of houses lying behind New Canal Street. There is a water tap in the centre, which would have been shared by several houses, along with communal toilets and washhouses where laundry was done.

Number 19 Northumberland Street, *c.* 1905. This house, which is in the process of demolition, shows signs of former grandeur. Graffiti are obviously not a recent phenomenon!

Numbers 10 to 14 Richard Street, *c.* 1905. One of the houses has a small shop displaying its wares in a bay window.

Rear of Rowland Street and Lawley Street, *c.* 1905. These houses must have been extremely unhealthy with their tiny windows.

The last horse tram in Nechells, 30 September 1906. The photographer was A. Twigg of Bloomsbury Street. Mr Wiggins was the driver and the house in the background belonged to Dr Cooper.

Numbers 1 to 6 in 3 Court, Landor Street, c. 1905. These houses were superior as they each had a patch of ground in front.

Number 35 Holt Street, *c.* 1905.

Holt Street, *c.* 1905. This open space between Lister Street and Oxygen Street was no doubt where some houses had recently been demolished. The advertisements are for HP Sauce and Lewis's Hats, amongst others. HP Sauce had its factory in Aston and Lewis's was a large department store in Birmingham, which also had branches in other towns.

Numbers 5, 6 and 7 in 4 Court, Lawford Street, 22 June 1907. Everyone has come outside to be photographed.

Number 24 Bullock Street, c. 1905. This strange dwelling looks as though it was converted from an old railway carriage. On the patch of ground at the back was a gypsy encampment complete with traditional caravans.

Numbers 7, 8 and 9 Fox Street, *c.* 1905.

Fazeley Street, *c.* 1905.

House at the back of No. 12 Glover Street, 28 June 1904. In spite of the poverty and poor housing conditions, the children look clean and well cared for. This would not have been easy with only an outside cold-water tap.

Number 5 Court, Dartmouth Street, c. 1905. The bricks have been whitewashed to reflect more light and efforts have been made to brighten it up with a window box and ornate gas lamp.

Numbers 1-16 Crawford Street, *c.* 1905. The backs of the houses are seen in this photograph, before they were repaired.

Numbers 1-16 Crawford Street, *c.* 1905. These are the same houses as in the last photograph, after they have been repaired.

Houses in the area before the building of Ashcroft Estate, Vauxhall, *c.* 1930. This was part of the Ministry of Health's 'five-year plan' to abolish all slums with the help of Government subsidies. The estate stands on the site of the Great Brook Street cavalry barracks.

The opening of the Ashcroft Estate by
the Prince of Wales, later Edward
VIII, 23 October, 1934. The estate's
name perpetuates that of Dr John
Ash, founder of the General Hospital.

The Prince of Wales on the occasion
of the opening of the Ashcroft Estate,
23 October 1934.

The opening of the Ashcroft Estate by the Prince of Wales, 23 October 1934.

Drawings for the Ashcroft Estate, 27 October 1932. The architect was H.H. Humphries and the builders were Henry Boot & Sons. The Ashcroft Estate is still in existence and all the maisonettes are now listed buildings.

Great Francis Street, 1938.

Bloomsbury Street, 26 February 1953. The Duddeston and Nechells Development Plan had been approved by the City Council in 1943, but Government approval was not granted until 1950. A huge clearance and rebuilding programme was set in motion which involved constructing a new road called Nechells Parkway.

Interior of a house in Bloomsbury Street, 1950s. Chimney-breast cupboards were typical features of small houses where every space needed to be utilized. The fireguard was a very necessary precaution with open fires.

Interior of a house in Bloomsbury Street showing cooking range, 1950s.

Nechells Place, 1968. During the miners' strike of February 1972, the Saltley Coke Depot made national headlines as the scene of a mass picket which resulted in the gates to the Depot being closed for public safety reasons by the police.

High Park Corner, Nechells Green, 30 November 1964. Wimbush's was a very well-known chain of local baker's shops.

Northumberland Street, 1950s. These old houses were in the Duddeston and Nechells Redevelopment Area, photographed before demolition. The roadway appears to be in a very bad state of repair.

Lord Street, Nechells Green, 19 November 1964. The building on the corner used to be the Prince of Wales pub. The house next door to it on the left of the photograph was the vicarage of St Lawrence's church. It is perhaps surprising to see a horse and cart on the streets of Birmingham as late as 1964.

Numbers 15 to 3 Lord Street, 19
November 1964.

Forster Street, 16 November 1964.
This shows a view of the court
between Nos 4 and 2.

Windsor Street, Nechells Green, 16 November 1964. This view is looking from the corner of Forster Street towards Great Brook Street. One of the new blocks of flats is visible on the right at the end of the street.

Brighton Place, Duddeston Mill Road, 5 September 1969. This was known locally as 'bums' puzzle' as the residents would remove the house numbers to confuse bailiffs or debt collectors with the result that they did not know which house was which.

Austin Street, 7 November 1970.

Nechells Parkway, 10 August 1965. The flats in this photograph have already been demolished.

Little Hall Road, 6 July 1959. Queen's Tower was the first multi-storey block of flats built in Birmingham and was opened by Harold Macmillan, then Minister of Housing, on 5 February 1954. The adjoining blocks are Home Tower and High Tower. On the whole, multi-storey living has not been a success and many tower blocks have already been demolished. These, however, have been retained and are now listed buildings.

The interior of a new dwelling on the Duddeston Estate, 1950s.

Six
Churches and Chapels

Church of St James-the-Less, Ashted, 1873. The church was founded in 1789, when Dr John Ash's house was converted into a chapel after his departure from Birmingham. A separate parish was created in 1853. The church was badly damaged during the Second World War and was demolished about 1956.

St James' chapel, Ashted. This old engraving shows the chapel before it was enlarged in 1835.

St James' church, Ashted, 1896.

Bishop. Ryder's church, Gem Street, c. 1895. Built to commemorate Henry Ryder, Bishop of Lichfield, who died in 1836, it was designed by Thomas Rickman and R.C. Hussey and was consecrated in 1838. The chancel was rebuilt in 1894 by J.A. Chatwin and the church was demolished in 1960.

St Matthew's church, Great Lister Street, Duddeston. The foundation stone was laid on 12 October 1839 by Lord Calthorpe. Because Duddeston was so sparsely populated at this time, the church was called 'St Matthew's in the Wilderness.' It was the first of five churches built by the Birmingham Church Building Society.

St Matthew's church, Duddeston, from Willis Street, 1896.

South-west view of St Matthew's church, 20 November 1946 after the loss of the spire.

Interior of St Matthew's church, 20 November 1946. The galleries were added in 1866.

St Matthew's church, 1960s. Some of the flats in the photograph have already been demolished, but the gas holders have been preserved.

The old St Matthew's Vicarage, 20 November 1946. The vicarage was damaged during an air raid in the Second World War.

St Anne's vicarage, Cato Street, Duddeston, c. 1912. Built in 1908 by the architect W.H. Bidlake, it was later used as St Matthew's vicarage. Unfortunately, it has now been demolished.

St Clement's church, Nechells Park Road, 1896. Designed by J.A. Chatwin, this church was consecrated in 1859.

The interior of St Clement's church, 11 December 1946.

St Catherine's church, Scholefield Street, Nechells. This church was designed by Osborn and Reading and consecrated in 1878. In 1945 it was closed and after 1951 it was demolished when the parish joined with St Matthew's.

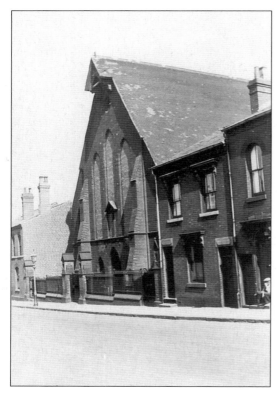

St Anne's church, Cato Street, Duddeston. This was a red-brick building designed by J.G. Dunn and consecrated in 1869. The church was closed in 1951.

Saltley Chapel. Situated near Saltley Hall, the chapel was for the resident family only and the general public had to go to St Peter and Paul's church, Aston, until their own church of St Saviour's was built.

St Saviour's church, Saltley, c. 1890. The architect was R.C. Hussey and the church was consecrated in 1850, the spire being added later.

St Peter's Mission church, Belmont Row, 11 December 1956.

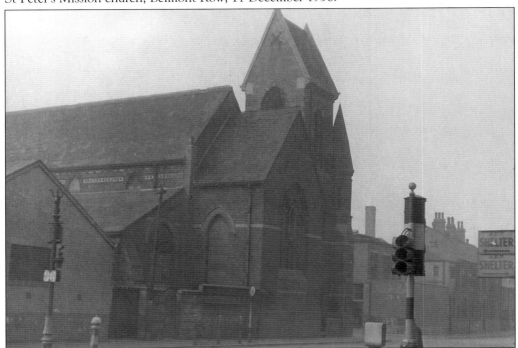

St Lawrence's church, Dartmouth Street, c. 1943. This was another church designed by J.A. Chatwin and built with the help of a £10,000 gift from Miss Louisa Ryland, one of Birmingham's most generous benefactors. It was consecrated in 1868 and closed in 1951, less than a century later. The signpost on the right points to the air-raid shelters provided for the civilian population during the Second World War.

Long Acre Methodist church, 11 December 1956. This chapel was built by the Primitive Methodists in 1854 as Long Acre Ebenezer chapel.

Nechells Wesleyan chapel, Nechells Park Road, c. 1890. Designed by W. Jenkins and built in 1863, this chapel replaced an earlier one opened in 1837. In 1929, the second chapel was declared unsafe and was replaced by a new one.

Saltley Baptist chapel, George Arthur Road. Built in 1894, this chapel is still in use today.

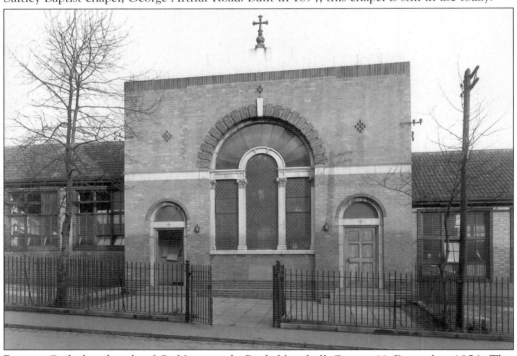

Roman Catholic church of St Vincent de Paul, Vauxhall Grove, 11 December 1956. This church was opened in 1930 and also served as a school hall. The mission had been established in 1883, however, along with St Vincent's Roman Catholic School.

Seven

Saltley

A view of Saltley, 1860. Although not a clear photograph, this view has been included as it is the earliest photograph of Saltley, showing its rural character before development. The growth of Saltley was largely due to Charles Bowyer Adderley, created the first Lord Norton in 1878, who inherited land in Saltley and elsewhere when he came of age in 1835. Lord Norton planned Saltley as a village with a new church and housing for working people. The population of Saltley grew from only a few hundred to 27,000 within his lifetime. A century later the area had deteriorated and the scheme was criticized for its overcrowding and poor building. However, in their day the houses were considered good examples of artisans' dwellings.

Numbers 92-96 Bridge Road, Saltley, c. 1905. These old cottages were about to be demolished at the time of this photograph.

Lord Norton, 1814-1905. Besides planning the development of Saltley, Lord Norton was well known as a politician, being MP for the northern division of Staffordshire from 1841 until 1878.

Numbers 11-13 Chapel Terrace,
Saltley Road, 1905.

Number 39 Adderley Road, Saltley,
c. 1912. According to the board
above the doorway, the licensee of
this 'outdoor' was Frederick Barber.
No doubt he is photographed here
with his family, the smaller of the
two boys resplendent in his sailor
suit.

Bridge Road, Saltley, June 1925.

Saltley Bridge, 1988. The London to Birmingham Railway has now been electrified.

Bridge Road, Saltley, 17 April 1923.

Bridge Road, Saltley, 16 July 1924.

Alum Rock Railway Bridge during reconstruction, 17 December 1932.

Highfield Road, Saltley.

High Street, Saltley, 17 May 1941. This photograph shows extensive bomb damage after an air raid during the Second World War.

Saltley railway station, looking south, *c.* 1912. This station was built in 1854 on the Birmingham and Derby Junction Railway line, which was opened in 1842 and became part of the Midland Railway in 1844.

Arley Road, showing the corner of Washwood Heath Road, early 1900s.

Devon Street, May 1978.

Eight
Public Buildings and Public Houses

A View of old Vauxhall Gardens, *c.* 1851. This watercolour by J.L. Pedley was done for the Victoria Building Society at the time the land was sold for building. It was exhibited in the window of the Society's offices in Union Street, Birmingham, for many years and was later purchased by Sir Benjamin Stone and taken to his house at Erdington, which was called The Grange. The original is now in Birmingham Museum and Art Gallery. Vauxhall Gardens was on the site of the old Duddeston Manor House, the seat of the Holte family before they moved to Aston Hall. The house on the right of the picture was called Vauxhall House.

The Gun Barrel Proof House, Banbury Street, 1813. The Proof House was established as the result of an Act of Parliament in order to regulate the testing of fire-arms. It is still in existence and is still used for its original purpose, although the famous Birmingham gun trade is now very much smaller than in its heyday.

Great Brook Street Barracks, 29 September 1932. The Church and King Riots of 1791 in which the houses of many Birmingham Dissenters were destroyed, gave the impetus to the building of the Great Brook Street Barracks in 1793. Four acres of land were acquired from Mr Brooke for the purpose. About this time, the Government was building barracks in many large towns so that soldiers would not have to be quartered in local inns. The barracks remained until the area was cleared for the building of the Ashcroft Estate.

Miss James' Almshouses, Nechells Park Road, 1896. The almshouses were erected in 1869 by the two spinster daughters of Mr John Howell James, one of the first two churchwardens of St Clement's church, Nechells. They were built to house thirty-one residents, widows, single women or married couples over the age of sixty. They have now been replaced by thirty modern flats. Several charities formed by the James family have now been brought together under the heading of the James Charities.

The Kyrle Hall, Sheep Street. Designed by W.H. Bidlake in 1893, the Kyrle Hall was built by the Kyrle Society, established in 1879 to perpetuate the memory of John Kyrle, sometimes known as the Man of Ross, who used his money to improve the town of Ross-on-Wye. The society's object was to bring natural and artistic beauty to the citizens of Birmingham. The Birmingham Guild of Handicraft developed out of this movement. The building was later used by the Birmingham Boys' and Girls' Union. In 1936 it was rebuilt, but in 1968 the land was needed for the expansion of Aston University and the hall was demolished.

Woodcock Street Baths. First opened in 1860, these were Birmingham's second public baths. A first-class swimming bath and a gala bath were added in 1926 after a rebuilding programme. These baths were familiar to generations of school children as it was a favourite venue for swimming sports and life-saving classes. It now forms part of Aston University's sports centre.

The interior of Woodcock Street Baths.

The interior of Woodcock Street Baths.

The interior of Saltley Baths, which were opened on a site behind the old police station in George Arthur Road on 30 July 1924. The architect was W.N. Twist.

Corporation Cottage Baths, Lower Dartmouth Street, *c.* 1914. Cottage baths were erected in areas of the city where most houses did not have bathrooms or, indeed, water laid on at all. Outside water taps were the usual source of water, which had to be heated in a copper for bathing and washing clothes.

Nechells Baths, Nechells Park Road, 1907. This photograph is from the *Builder's Journal*, 13 November 1907. The baths were opened by the Lord Mayor, Alderman W.H. Bowater, on 22 June 1910.

Norton Baths, Saltley, *c.* 1923. These cottage baths in Adderley Road were opened on 13 June 1923.

A later view of Norton Baths.

The old Saltley police station in George Arthur Road, early 1900s.

Adderley Park Library, 1913. Lord Norton erected this building in Adderley Park as a public library and museum. It was opened as a free library on 11 January 1864 and was run by the Birmingham Council although situated outside the borough at that time. The museum was not a success and the exhibits were transferred to Aston Hall.

Reading room at Adderley Park Library, 1911.

Adderley Park Library prior to demolition in 1965.

Bloomsbury Library, 1910. The newsroom opened on 4 June 1892 and the library on 29 September 1892. The architects of this distinctive terracotta brick building were Cossins and Peacock. The library is still flourishing today.

The interior of Bloomsbury Library, 1910.

The lending department of Bloomsbury Library, 1930s.

The lending department of Bloomsbury Library, 1930s.

Adderley Park, 5 August 1966. Adderley Park, Saltley, was leased to Birmingham Council at a peppercorn rent from Lord Norton and opened on 30 August 1856. Although outside the boundary at that time, it was Birmingham's first public park, still in use today.

The New Ashted Row cinema, 11 December 1956. Opened in 1912 as Ashted Row Picture Palace, the cinema was renovated and renamed in 1934. It was closed about 1958 and demolished.

The Delicia cinema, Gosta Green, 6 February 1951. Designed by the architects James and Lister Lea & Sons, the Delicia opened on 5 November 1923. In 1944 it closed as a cinema and was used for wrestling matches, without much success. In the mid-1960s, it was used by the BBC as TV studios and in the 1970s it became Aston University's Centre for the Arts, later the Triangle Arts Centre. This closed in the 1980s and the site is now occupied by Waterstone's bookshop. An old water trough for horses is in the bottom left corner of the photograph.

The interior of the Delicia Cinema, 22 May 1951. The cinema's conversion into a stadium for wrestling matches had already taken place at the time of this photograph.

Phoenix public house, Park Street, 1867. The Murphy anti-Catholic riots took place only two or three days before. One of the houses on the right shows evidence of damage.

The Old Nelson Inn on the corner of Great Lister Street and Rupert Street, 1960s.

The Junction Inn on the corner of Great Francis Street, *c*. 1890. The two men on the left in uniform are tram drivers and a tram is just approaching.

Another view of the Junction Inn, 2 August 1963.

The Raven Inn, Great Lister Street, 19 November 1964.

The Swan, Bloomsbury Street, 12 July 1962. The tower of Loxton Street School is visible on the right of the photograph.

Nechells Green Community Centre, 1960s.

Moor Street Station, 8 September 1951. A new station has now been built alongside the old one.

Curzon Street station, *c.* 1838. This station was the Birmingham terminus of the London to Birmingham Railway. The London terminus was the Euston Arch, whose demolition caused such a furore. Curzon Street was only in use as a passenger station for a few years as it was too far from the town centre. When New Street station was completed in 1852, the trains from London terminated there instead.

Curzon Street goods yard, April 1857. Curzon Street station with its adjacent hotel can be seen at the bottom left of the photograph.

The hotel next to Curzon Street station, 19 June 1971. The building was demolished soon after this time.

The interior of Curzon Street station, August 1969.

Curzon Street station on a sunny summer's day, 19 August 1932. This station building forms the focus of the Millenium Point development, which includes the new Science Museum, to be called the ThinkTank. With this development, the eastern sector of Birmingham looks back to its past and forward to its exciting new future.